Budgeting: How to Budget Your Money?

Book 3 of Money: Learning the Basics

Joseph Evaldi

The Books from the Series
Money: Learning the Basics

Going Broke: Learning from Financial Mistakes (Money: Learning the Basics Book 1)

Saving: How to Save Your Money (Money: Learning the Basics Book 2)

Budgeting: How to Budget Your Money (Money: Learning the Basics Book 3)

Retirement: Start Thinking About Your Retirement (Money: Learning the Basics Book 4)

Disclaimer

Otherwise, have fun reading this book. I hope it gives you some ideas that you can use.

Table of Contents

Acknowledgements

I would like to thank the books that I've read about budgeting. They were a great help to me.

I would also like to thank the videos that I have watched on YouTube. They were also a great help to me.

Last and foremost I want to thank my family and the woman I will marry. They have been a great support to me and have taught me valuable means about budgeting.

Introduction

In the first book I discussed about the facts of going broke. The second book I discussed about the importance of saving money. This is the third book in a series of books. In this book I discuss about the importance of budgeting.

Budgeting is debated by people. Some may think it is the next best thing since sliced bread and others may just hate it. Either way budgeting can be an asset if it is used right even if you don't like it.

Like saving money it is a disciplinary tactic that can be used.

What is Budgeting?

Budgeting is where you limit yourself a certain amount a week and stick to the budget. There are benefits to this if you do it. However, there also is a down side to it. Sometimes you might feel limited. All of these points will be discussed in this book.

What will be discussed in this Book?

The first chapter of the book, I will discuss about dividing your check when you are on a budget. The second chapter I will discuss about the importance of living on a budget and sticking to it.

The third chapter I will discuss about resisting the urge of spending your money and rewarding yourself for sticking to the budget.

The fourth chapter I will discuss about the techniques you can use for setting a budget rather it's handwritten or on Excel

In the fifth chapter, I discuss about automating your budget. So that way you could spend and not worry about it.

Then I discuss about how you know your budget is working and finally wrapping up about the topic on budgeting.

Advice about Reading this Book

This book on budgeting is to give you pointer of what I learned about budgeting. I will tell you what has worked for me and what hasn't. I will also tell you like I told you in the last book that this book is to reinforce these ideas on budgeting into me.

If you follow these tips or are already using them,

great. If you're just picking up tips on this book, then this book is for you. However, if you don't like this book and don't want to budget, than that is your decision to make. I am not going to change your decision one way or the other. I just want to add an alternative view. I hope you enjoy and learn all you can read. Enjoy this book.

1

Dividing Your Check and Setting a Budget

It's good to know how much you are spending and where that money is going in order to set a budget. The essentials need to be set.

Every budget is different. From this video by Kendra Atkins, https://www.youtube.com/watch?v=S2ASPqEgV8g, it discusses about the importance of writing down all your expenses, debts, bills, etc. and then work of the list to pay it off. The guy in the video say if you have all your credit card debt or debt, pay the minimum on all of them and then chip away at the smallest debt and it will snowball.

I agree with this. It is a plan for budgeting. Also, by dividing it up you are making sure what is important is getting paid. And the good thing is you could play around with the numbers.

What I do with my budget now is spend for $30 a week for gas now that gas for the car has dropped. I have my phone bill, and my credit card bill. And I am living at home until I could afford to live on my own and then I will adopt other expenses that I will take on.

The key is allocating your money and having some left

over so it can accumulate and setting some money aside so you could spend for the week and enjoy some as well.

Whatever, your expenses are it is good to divide or allocate your check and like I said play around with your numbers. Whatever plan you choose, it's the best plan for you. Rather you give yourself $40 spending money per week or $60. It is up to you, but I will get to that in the next chapter.

2

Setting a Budget and Sticking to It

It is debated rather you want to stick to a budget. David Bach says that it is good to automate your expenses, your bills, and your savings and you could spend the rest. However, I feel that knowing what you are spending and limiting yourself to that amount, then that might help you be cautious of your spending habits.

What I usually do is give myself between $40 and $60 spending money for the week and then when that money goes I try not to spend what's in the bank.

It might be difficult to do and it might not be ideal to stick with it. I know I've broken the system many times, but I know when I'm on the system it works.

I know there might be overlap, but the key is to stay with the budget.

Everybody has expenses and you should have fun with your money.

I make time for fun. I enjoy having coffee so I budget that in with my expenses. I know there are ways of saving money, but what good is it if you can't enjoy it. This is what a budget should be.

You might feel restricted with a budget and as I've heard it will help you think about what you are spending, but eventually it will pay off and if you put some of that money aside for your fun fund, then you will enjoy your money.

However, the bottom line is that you set a limit and stick to it. Don't worry, if you are not perfect, it takes time to practice, but you will get there.

In the next chapter, I will discuss about resisting the urge to over spend while you are on a budget.

3

Resisting the Urge to Overspend While on a Budget

There are always impulse expenditures and you should set money aside for that in the budget. Those expenses should not go on the credit card.

This is what people do. They buy off impulse and rack up the debt. That is why it is helpful to resist the urge of temptation. I know it's easier said than done, but not putting that money on the credit card unless you necessarily have to will save you a lot of headaches in the long run.

There are benefits in doing this. Once you've become disciplined it is like habit forming and you will be doing it without thinking. The same is true with bad habits. That is why it is important to train yourself.

I don't mean not spending at all and being frugal. What good is money if you can't spend it, but it doesn't mean carelessly spending it? There are things to do without or cutting back on.

It is up to you on what to budget on. And I don't have to give you a lecture on your expenses, even though it might be helpful to you. It is good to know what you could spend your money on and it ties in with last chapter. I don't need to go in great detail. You know your expenses better than anybody else.

In the next chapter, I will write about the systems you could use for budgeting, writing it down or using Microsoft Excel.

4

What Method do you Use to Budget?

With Budgeting, there are fun things you can do. You can either use a Microsoft Excel program or you could hand write it. In this chapter I will discuss the pros and cons of both.

Handwritten

With hand writing it the pros are that it is easier to do. You could have a special designed notebook dedicated to your budgeting and you could map out how and where you will allocate your expenses. You can choose whatever notepad you are going to do it on. I prefer this to Microsoft Excel, but there are benefits to that to.

The cons of it being handwritten are when you make a mistake you have to do it over again or you have to scratch it out.

Microsoft Excel

There are good things about Microsoft Excel if you

have it. You can keep it organized and write down your expenses. You will know when you are paying for a bill and when. This is the benefits of Microsoft Excel.

On the downside it could be confusing to add up the amount. Unless you know how Excel works, calculating it might not be easy to do.

Also, you have to remind yourself to check your page and try to update it after awhile.

Apps for the Tablet

Apps for the Tablet are a great way to track your spending. They could be from your bank that will help or other companies. You have to price it out. Some will cost money and some will not.

These are a great way to visually see what you have or own and it helps you to think or strategize what you want to do with your money. This technique will help.

I prefer to do it the old fashion way, but you could do whatever way works for you. It could be an asset to know where your expenses are going.

In the next chapter, I discuss about automating your expenses.

5

<u>Automating It</u>

In this chapter, I discuss about automating it. David Bach suggests that you have a system where 10% goes towards retirement, 5% goes towards your emergency fund, and other expenses such as bills should go towards an automated system where it is done automatically.

This can be done so you don't have to worry about it. You just have to be sure to keep that amount in your bank so it could be sent or after you get paid you could have it sent.

People who are successful automated, but it's truly your choice on what to do. Rather you have a system in place so you could make your payments when you are sick or you do it yourself. This is something to think of.

In the next chapter, I will be wrapping up this short book on budgeting.

Conclusion

Good Budgeting is allocation of your funds and there are different ways you can budget. Rather you are limiting yourself a certain amount a week or you are automating your funds. Either way, the choice is up to you.

Only you know your fixed expenses and your other expenses and as I learned from reading Tony Robbins new book <u>**MONEY Master the Game: 7 Simple Steps to Financial Freedom**</u> it might be beneficial financially to move to a different environment. Maybe you need a change in life and this could help you with your living expenses.

We are ingrained that we are comfortable with our situation when a change is something that can be beneficial for us. We shouldn't be limited. This is the same with a budget to. Even though we may feel we are restricted. Are we?

We delay the gratification and use it for a time when we need it. Many of us don't think like this. I didn't think like this until recently and as Tony Robbins states in the title of his book Money Master the Game. It is a game to be played and there are many ways to play it. Budgeting is only a small part of it.

Sticking to a budget is discipline and you want to plan

in your budget some fun to. What's good about money if we can't enjoy it? It is the same about life. We work very hard at it and we work, but seldom do we ever enjoy life. We are always moving on to the next thing and never appreciating what life offers us and we react on impulse at times to give us the fix we need at that time. This is why it is important to budget in money for fun.

We need to enjoy the life we have and money is an extension of it. In budgeting we incorporate strategy, discipline, and the comfort of knowing that your bills will be paid.

We want a good life and these are the things we do. I know everyone allocates their funds. There is no right or wrong with budgeting. And it is your choice if you want to automate your funds. Whatever way, budgeting is what you make of it. Make the best of it.

Preview

Retirement: Start Thinking About Your Retirement (Money: Learning the Basics Book 4)

Introduction

I am 35 years old and I am approaching 36 years old at this time of this writing. Retirement is 30 years away from me. It's safe to say I have to think about retirement. Like many I didn't plan my future and I lived for the day. I am just lucky enough to have $8,500 saved in my finances.

That is why I am writing this book. I am not screwed yet. I could make decisions that will change my life. And this book can help you to think about retirement like I am now.

In this book I will discuss about the options you have

for retirement. I did research on retirement, but I am sad to say I haven't done it fully. However, I am going to discuss what I have learned about retirement.

Many young people like me didn't think about their retirement, they live for today or they planned for the future and they lost their money in 2008 during the crash.

I didn't plan on my future, I just planned here and there and I've been working in two jobs that give me two days a week at the time of this writing. After I left one job, the other job is giving me more hours. This is a reason why I embarked in side hustle with writing.

The fact is when you get older you think more about the future and your older years. There are many options I plan on doing for the future and all we know is that the future is uncertain. That is why no matter where you are in your investment life, 18 years old and starting or 55 years old and ready to retire. There is a chance to develop a plan for the future where you can succeed in your retirement years.

What I won't talk about in this book?

I won't talk about where you should put your money. That is your choice. I will give you suggestions of where it can go that can help you no matter what age you are.

I won't talk about numbers and figures because they can be intimidating even though some numbers are smaller then it seems. Anything can make money, but the idea of compounding will do a lot more and it isn't that much to make much when you think of it.

And I won't discuss about risky investments even though in times such as depression everything is a risk which I will discuss about in Chapter 1.

A Run Down of the Chapters in the Book

In the first chapter, I will discuss about times of financial depression. There are things to do in times of financial stress. Maybe we lost our money from bad investments, or our investment just crashed, or we didn't spend wisely our money. And as time went on we are later at life and we don't know what to do. Some people play the catch up game. This will be discussed.

In Chapter 2, I discuss about not putting all your eggs in one basket. You can't bank on putting all of your money in one place. This will lead you up shits creek and then 1929 or 2008 happened. For people not prepared for the storm, it will hurt in your pockets.

In the Third Chapter, I will discuss about the pros and

the cons of the 401(K) or the 403(B). Should we put all our trust in them?

In Chapter 4, I discuss about the different retirement investment options such as IRAs, Insurance, Bonds and Emergency Savings. There needs to be preparation when you retire.

In the Fifth Chapter, I discuss making your money work for you even into retirement. This is the idea of royalties'. Money you can make long after you're gone.

In the Sixth Chapter, I will discuss about setting up your money for your loved ones until after you're gone.

Then in the last chapter, I will wrap up the topics in this book and discuss what to do with retirement. This is a time where you grow old. How do you want to spend it? As I watched in a documentary movie like The Secret, they raised the question, what will your Opus be? In other words, how will you leave your mark on this earth? How will others learn from you?

I raise that question here because after a full life of work and experience in and out of your job, there is something to offer. What will be remembered of you until after you're gone? What mark have you left for others?

This is important and a chapter in itself. Retirement is something to think about and as the promo setting up

Wrestlemania 31 between the Undertaker and Bray Wyatt. The Undertakers words were, "I'm not dead yet." He was saying, he might be beaten, but still he has a lot more to offer.

Life is like this. The Baby Boomers are the wealthiest demographic in the Country and even though the young try to move them over, they work and hold onto their spot even more so then the young and ambitious.

The idea of retirement has changed. Who would have thought 20 years later since the internet came on the scene, 11 years after Facebook, and a few years after Twitter; the baby boomers now complain that they don't have a smart phone for them. This is a changing world and thinking about retirement is different. It is a time where you reacquaint with your friends and prepare for your journey home.

I don't mean to make it sound doom and gloom, but you want to make the most of your retirement. Some work until they die and some enjoy life for a span of 20 years. This will be the final chapter in the book.

Retirement is your decision. It is up to you to decide what you want to do with your life. I wish you the best in making your decision.

References

Bach, David. *The Automatic Millionaire*. 2004. Broadway Books: New York.

Robbins, Tony. *Money Master the Game 7 Simple Steps to Financial Freedom*. 2014. Simon & Schuster: New York.

Books Written By Joseph Evaldi

Fiction

A Soul Warrior's Journey

The Day at the Bismarck Herald: The Newspaper Reporter War

Christmas Fiction

Finding Christmas: The Story of Joseph

Non-Fiction

Birth Order: How the Roles of Each Sibling are Placed at Birth?

The World of Groups: Sociology and My Experiences in Senior Seminar

The Amazing Effects of Water

The Enlightened Way: How the Zen Path Can Help Treat Depression?

Applying Your Own Interests to Your Boring Job: Can It Be Done?

Poetry

Apparitions of a Warrior

Websites for Joseph Evaldi

http://www.facebook.com/Josephevaldi

https://www.youtube.com/channel/UCSp2TBz566yOGiQfLf
k0Zog

http://www.twitter.com/passageofjoe

http://www.amazon.com/Joseph-
Evaldi/e/B00ONSPVQI/ref=sr_ntt_srch_lnk_1?qid=14179608
24&sr=8-1

About the Author

Joseph Evaldi graduated from Kean University studying Sociology. He ventured in with writing with his book **The Amazing Effects of Water** in 2009.

He then wrote his first novel **A Soul Warrior's Journey** in April 2013. He later finished writing a book of poetry called **Apparitions of a Warrior** in July 2013.

In December 2014, The Amazon Kindle book **Birth Order: How the Roles of Each Sibling are Placed at Birth?** Was the hot new release under Sociology of Marriage & Family for Amazon.

He is currently working on a string of short ebooks which will be released on Amazon Kindle this year.